SPECTRUM®
READERS

LEVEL 1

IMPORTANT!

By Teresa Domnauer

Carson-Dellosa
Publishing

SPECTRUM®

An imprint of Carson-Dellosa Publishing, LLC
P.O. Box 35665
Greensboro, NC 27425-5665

carsondellosa.com

Printed in the USA. All rights reserved.
ISBN 978-1-4838-0117-9

01-002141120

What do workers do each day?
They care for others.
They make useful things.
They provide services
people need.
What job will you do someday?

Dentist

Dentists have important jobs. They check teeth to make sure they are healthy. They fix teeth that are hurting.

Police Officer

Police officers have
important jobs.
They patrol streets
and fight crime.
They keep people safe.

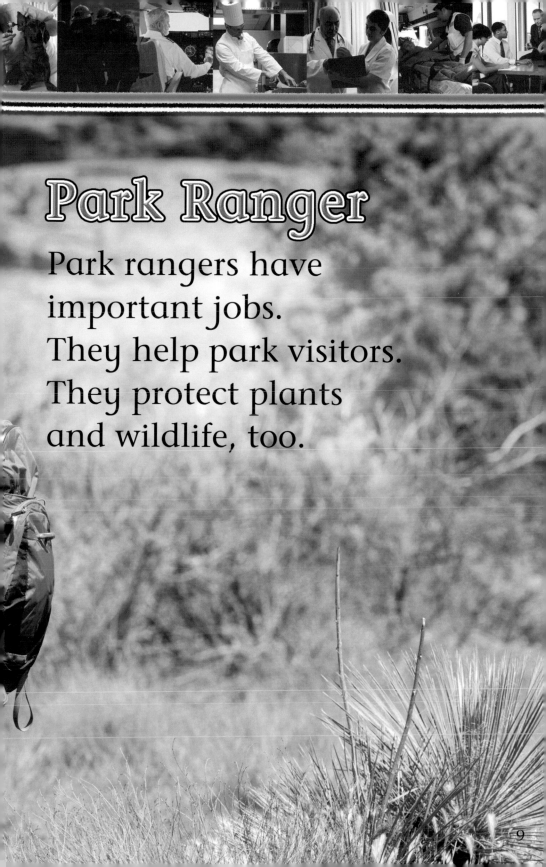

Park Ranger

Park rangers have important jobs. They help park visitors. They protect plants and wildlife, too.

Teacher

Teachers have
important jobs.
They help students learn.
They make school
safe and fun.

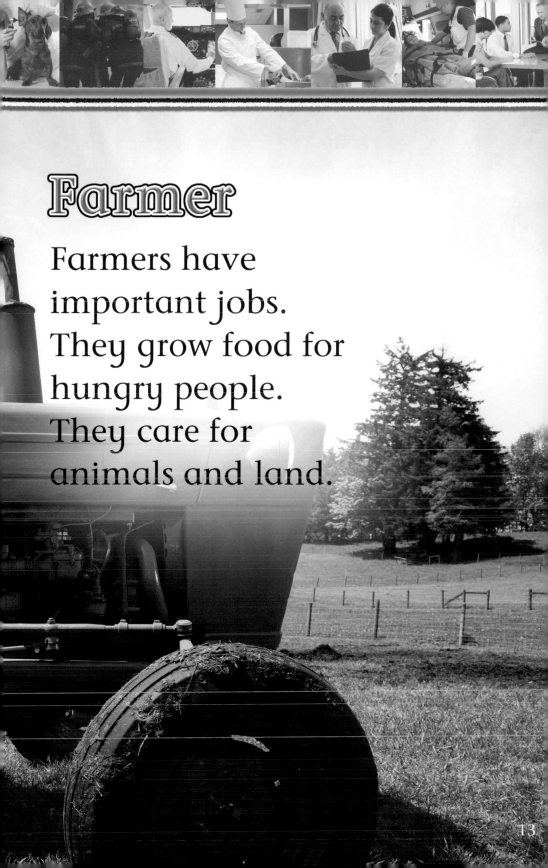

Farmer

Farmers have
important jobs.
They grow food for
hungry people.
They care for
animals and land.

Construction Worker

Construction workers have important jobs. They make houses and other buildings. They build roads and bridges, too.

Scientist

Scientists have
important jobs.
They ask questions
and do experiments.
Their discoveries
help people.

Veterinarian

Veterinarians have
important jobs.
They keep animals healthy.
They help sick animals
feel better, too.

Firefighter

Firefighters have important jobs. They put out dangerous fires. They rescue people and animals from fires, too.

Airline Pilot

Airline pilots have
important jobs.
They fly planes with
great skill.
They help people
travel safely.

Chef

Chefs have important jobs. They prepare all kinds of food. They create delicious meals.

Doctor and Nurse

Doctors and nurses
have important jobs.
They help sick
people get well.
They save
people's lives.

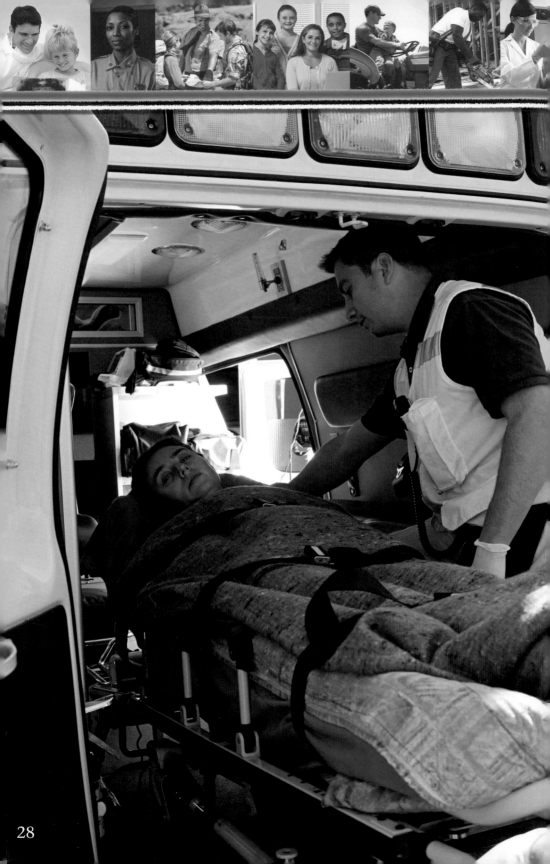

EMT

Emergency medical technicians have important jobs. They drive ambulances to emergencies. They quickly help people who are hurt.

Business Person

Business people have important jobs.
They work together in offices.
They manage companies that sell things people need.

IMPORTANT! Jobs Comprehension Questions

1. What do the letters in EMT stand for?

2. What are a teacher's responsibilities?

3. Who do veterinarians care for?

4. What do farmers do?

5. How does a scientist make discoveries?

6. Where do business people work?

7. Why are doctors important?

8. What does an airline pilot do?

9. Name two things that construction workers build.

10. How do police officers help people?

11. Name two more jobs people do.

12. What job would you like to do? Why?